Small Graveyards & Burial Grounds: Kingston, Ontario, Canada

The Grave Whisperer

Angeline Gallant

Published by Angeline Gallant, 2022.

SMALL GRAVEYARDS & BURIAL GROUNDS: KINGSTON, ONTARIO, CANADA

First edition. September 20, 2022.

Copyright © 2022 Angeline Gallant.

ISBN: 979-8215953662

Written by Angeline Gallant.

Also by Angeline Gallant

Calling Her Heart
Whisper of the Heart
No Turning Back
Forsake Me Not
Hear My Cry

Keeper Of Secrets
A Lady's Secret

Midnight's Awakening
Heart of the Storm
Walking Through The Storm

Secrets of the Underworld
Deklan's Dragons

Tell My Story Collection

Tell My Story: England 1852

The Grave Whisperer
Wedding Bells in Kingston, Ontario, Canada 1923
St. Paul's Anglican Churchyard Kingston, Ontario, Canada A-B
St. Paul's Anglican Churchyard, Kingston, Ontario, Canada C - D
St. Paul's Anglican Churchyard, Kingston, Ontario, Canada G - H
St. Paul's Anglican Churchyard, Kingston, Ontario, Canada J - N
St. Paul's Anglican Churchyard, Kingston, Ontario, Canada O - R
St. Paul's Anglican Churchyard, Kingston, Ontario, Canada S - T
St. Paul's Anglican Churchyard, Kingston, Ontario T - Z
Small Graveyards & Burial Grounds: Kingston, Ontario, Canada

The Wolf Whisperer Series
The Cry of the Wolf
Journey of the Heart
Wolf Whisperer volumes 1 & 2

Standalone
Winds of Change vol 1-3

Watch for more at https://www.goodreads.com/author/show/
19703964.Angeline_Gallant.

Table of Contents

BUCK CEMETERY

CATHARINE (HAEFNER) BUCK[1]

Catharine was born in Germany on July 9, 1841 and was christened on July 18th.

She was two years old when her brother, Franz, passed away in 1843.

Catharine was three years old when her brother, Fredericke, passed away in 1844.

She was 17 years old then she married Thomas George Buck Sr. on January 25, 1859.

She was 25 years old when Ontario was founded on July 1, 1867.

Catharine was 29 years old when British Columbia joined the confederation in 1871.

She was 41 years old when the mining boom in Northern Ontario took place in 1883.

Catharine was 67 years old when her husband passed away on December 8, 1908.

She was 70 years old when her brother, Eckhard, passed away in 1912.

Catharine was 72 years old when Germany declared war on Russia on August 1, 1914.

She was 76 years old when her brother, Johann Christian, passed away in 1917 and when World War I ended in 1918. Her brother Wilhelm William passed away on January 9th and she passed away two months later on March 16th.

GEORGE BUCK JR. E.U.[2]

George was born in Kingston, Frontenac, Upper Canada, British Colonial America, on December 22, 1796.

He was 15 years old when he served in the flank corps during the War of 1812.

George was 27 years old when he married Pheobe in Lansdowne, Ontario in 1824.

He was 41 years old when his brother, Adam, passed away in 1838.

George was 59 years old when his father passed away in 1856.

He was 65 years old when his brother, Philip, passed away in 1862.

George was 67 years old when his mother passed away in 1864.

He was 73 years old when his sister, Elizabeth, passed away in 1870.

George was 74 years old when British Columbia joined the confederation in 1871. His sister, Catherine, passed away on May 8th.

He was 82 years old when he passed away on January 13, 1879, the same day as his brother, Martin.

THOMAS GEORGE BUCK SR. [3]

Thomas was born on January 22, 1835 in Kingston, Ontario.

He was 24 years old when he married Catharine on January 25, 1859 in Frontenac, Ontario.

Thomas was 31 years old when Ontario was founded on July 1, 1867.

He was 44 years old when his father passed away in 1879.

Thomas was 47 years old when the mining boom in northern Ontario began in 1883.

He was 58 years old when his mother passed away in 1894.

Thomas was 67 years old when his brother, George Henry, passed away in 1902.

He was 73 years old when he passed away on December 8, 1908.

CALEB FAIRBANKS JR.[4]

Caleb was born on June 3, 1790 in Boston, Massachusetts.

He was 21 years old when the War of 1812 took place. Caleb served in the military.

Caleb was 24 years old when he married Nancy on June 1, 1814 in Lisbon, New York.

He was 38 years old when his son, James, passed away on August 25, 1828. Caleb's sister, Mary, passed away on March 29, 1829.

Caleb was 41 years old when his brother, James, passed away in 1832.

He was 42 years old when his brother, Ephriam, passed away in 1833.

Caleb was 47 years old when his sister, Hannah, passed away on August 7, 1837. His infant son, Christopher Isaac, passed away four months later on December 9th.

He was 51 years old when his father passed away in 1842.

Caleb was 65 years old when his daughter, Jane, passed away in 1856.

He was 66 years old when his mother passed away a few months later in 1856.

Caleb was 68 years old when his brother, Dexter, passed away in 1858.

He was 75 years old when his sister, Betsey, passed away in 1865.

Caleb was 76 years old when his brother, Jabez, passed away in 1866.

He was 77 years old when he passed away on September 25, 1867.

CLARISSA (FAIRBANKS) WRIGHT[5]

Clarissa was born on December 16, 1839 in Kingston, Frontenac, Canada West, British Colonial America. She was Dutch.

She was three years old when "A Christmas Carol" was first published.

Clarissa was 16 years old when her sister, Jane, passed away in 1856.

She was 27 years old when Ontario was founded on July 1, 1867. Her father passed away two months later on September 25th.

Clarissa was 43 years old when the mining boom in Northern Ontario began in 1883.

She was 48 years old when her brother, William James, passed away in 1888.

Clarissa was 49 years old and Methodist when she passed away on October 18, 1889.

McBURNEY (SKELETON) PARK

MARY McLEOD[6]

Mary was born in 1807.

She was 27 years old when she passed away in 1834. A park was built over her grave.

ELEONORE "LEONORA" (BEDARD) PERRY[7]

Leonora was born on August 26, 1816 in Kingston, Frontenac, Upper Canada, British Colonial America. She was French. She was 33 years old when she passed away on June 26, 1850.

PAUL PERRY[8]

Paul was married to Leonora and was a ship carpenter.
He passed away on July 28, 1851. A park was built over his grave.

WELLBORN & GLAZEBY BURIAL MOUND

JOHN GLAZEBY[9]

John was born in 1760.

He was 31 years old when the first parliament of Upper Canada assembled on September 17, 1791.

John was 80 years old when he passed away in 1840.

ANNE WELLBORN[10]

Anne was born in 1823.
She was 31 years old when she passed away in 1854.

MARMADUKE WELLBORN[11]

Marmaduke was born in England on July 26, 1787. He was christened in Wetwang, Yorkshire, England, on July 30th.

Marmaduke was 25 years old when he married Mary Ranson on December 12, 1812 in Wetwang, England.

He was 33 years old when his father passed away in 1821.

Marmaduke was 47 years old when his mother passed away in 1835.

He was 59 years old when his wife passed away in 1846.

Marmaduke was 66 years old when his brother, Jesse, passed away in 1853.

He was 75 years old when the battle at Gettysburg took place in 1863.

Marmaduke was 76 years old when he passed away on July 10, 1863 in Kingston, Frontenac, Canada West, British Colonial America.

MARY (RANSON) WELLBORN[12]

Mary was born in England on July 3, 1791.

She was 21 years old when she married Marmaduke on December 12, 1812 in Wetwang, Yorkshire, England.

Mary was 23 years old when Napoleon Boneparte was defeated in 1815.

She was 55 years old when she passed away on July 25, 1846.

KINGSTON PROVINCIAL PENITENTIARY CEMETERY

JANE CHARLOTTE (HAWKINS) McCORMICK[13]

Jane was born in 1843.

She was 24 years old when Ontario was founded on July 1, 1867.

Jane was 28 years old when British Columbia joined the confederation in 1871.

She was 70 years old when she passed away on March 2, 1913.

MATTHEW UDELL[14]

Matthew was born in 1804.

He was 21 years old when he married Mary on May 3, 1825 in Markham, Ontario.

Matthew was 44 years old when he passed away while in prison on September 1, 1848.

McBURNEY PARK (OLD ST. MARY CEMETERY)

ALICIA ELIZABETH "ALICE" (LESTER) FOWLER[15]

Alice was born in Dungarvan, Ireland in 1775.

She was 38 years old when she married Patrick in Kilkenny, Ireland in 1813.

Alice was 72 years old when her husband passed away in 1847.

She was 87 years old when her son, William, passed away in 1862.

Alice was 90 years old when her daughter, Alice, passed away in 1865.

She was 92 when her daughter, Mary, passed away in 1867.

Alice was 96 years old when her daughter, Ellen, passed away in 1871.

She was 100 years old when her daughter, Catherine, passed away in 1875.

Alice was 103 years old when her son, Martin, passed away in 1878.

She was 104 years old when she passed away on October 3, 1879. A park was built over her grave.

DENNIS FOWLER[16]

Dennis was born in 1831. It is uncertain when he died, however, a park was built over his grave in Kingston, Ontario.

ELLEN FOWLER[17]

Ellen was born in 1826. It is uncertain when she passed away. A park was built over her grave.

PATRICK FOWLER[18]

Patrick was born in County Kilkenny, Ireland in 1785.

He was 12 years old when The Battle of Antrim took place and the Young Ireland rebellion failed in 1798.

Patrick was 27 years old when he married Alice in Kilkenny in 1813.

He was 59 years old when the Irish Potato Famine took place in 1845.

Patrick was 61 years old when he passed away on June 7, 1847.

A park was built over his grave.

THOMAS FOWLER[19]

THOMAS WAS BORN IN 1824. It is unknown when he died.

JEREMIAH O'CONNOR[20]

Jeremiah was born in Ireland in 1808.

He was 22 years old when he married Mary Fowler on February 21, 1830 in Kingston, Upper Canada.

Jeremiah was 34 years old when he passed away on August 16, 1842.

ST. MARY'S ROMAN CATHOLIC CATHEDRAL & CRYPT

SISTER MARY AUSTIN[21]

Mary was a nun when she passed away on March 11, 1880. She is buried in the crypt.

LINDA BRAZZONI[22]

Linda was born on September 10, 1930.

She was three years old when the Dionne Quintuplets were born in 1934.

Linda was 51 years old when the Canada Act was passed in 1981.

She was 91 years old when she passed away on March 28, 2022.

ANNIE (COMPEAU) BUCK[23]

Annie was born in December 1892.

She was 13 years old when Hydro-Electric was established in Ontario in 1906.

Annie was 27 years old when she married Joseph Buck on January 29, 1920 in Kingston.

She was 28 years old when her sister, Julia Helena, passed away on December 24, 1920.

Annie was 41 years old when the Dionne Quintuplets were born in 1934.

She was 42 years old when her brother, Joseph Hubert, passed away in 1935.

Annie was 80 years old when she passed away on December 3, 1972.

M. CATHERINE "KAY" BUCK[24]

Kay was born in 1927.

She was seven years old when the Dionne Quintuplets were born in 1934.

Kay was 55 years old when the Canada Act was passed in 1982.

She was 65 years old when she passed away on December 16, 1991.

SISTER CATHERINE BYRNE[25]

Catherine was a nun when she passed away on April 18, 1871.

SISTER SARAH BYRNE[26]

S arah was a nun when she passed away on April 7, 1870.

DAVID PATRICK CAMPBELL[27]

David was born in 1919.

He was 16 years old when the Dionne Quintuplets were born in 1934.

David was 64 years old when the Canada Act was passed in 1982.

He was 82 years old when he passed away on February 20, 2000.

DORIS MAE (TISDALE) CAMPBELL[28]

Doris was born in 1920.

She was 14 years old when the Dionne Quintuplets were born in 1934.

Doris was 62 years old when the Canada Act was passed in 1982.

She was 73 years old when she passed away on October 17, 1993.

BISHOP JAMES VINCENT CLEARY[29]

James was born on September 18, 1828 in Dungarvan, County Waterford, Ireland.

He was 10 years old when The Night of the Big Wind took place in 1839.

James was 16 years old when the Irish Potato Famine took place in 1845.

He was 30 years old when his mother passed away in 1858.

James was 38 years old when Ontario was founded on July 1, 1867.

He was 42 years old when his father passed away in 1871.

James served as a bishop in Kingston, Ontario. *(Please see footnote for more resources)*

He was 69 years old when he passed away on February 24, 1898.

GARY F. COMPEAU[30]

G ary passed away on April 6, 1991.

JOSEPH HUBERT COMPEAU[31]

Joseph was born on May 5, 1902 on Garden Island, Frontenac, Ontario.

He was three years old when Ontario Hydro was established in 1906.

Joseph was 18 years old when his sister, Julia Helena, passed away in 1920.

He was 31 years old when the Dionne Quintuplets were born in 1934.

Joseph was 33 years old when he passed away on October 26, 1935.

MARGARET JEAN (TISDALE) COMPEAU[32]

Margaret was born in Canada in 1920.

She immigrated to the United States in 1921.

Margaret was two years old when her brother, John, passed away in 1922.

She was six years old when her sisters, Anna and Mary, both passed away on April 20, 1927. Her sister, Jean, passed away the following day on April 21st.

Margaret was 52 years old when her husband, Edward Milton, passed away in 1952.

She was 59 years old when the Refugee Act was passed in 1980.

MARGARET WAS 63 YEARS old when she passed away according to her gravestone inscription.

EDMOND MILTON COMPEAU[33]

Edmond was born on October 20, 1905 on Garden Island, Frontenac, Ontario.

He was 15 years old when his sister, Julia Helena, passed away in 1920.

Edmond was 20 years old when he immigrated to the United States on May 2, 1926.

He was 28 years old when the Dionne Quintuplets were born in 1934.

Edmond was 30 years old when his brother, Joseph Hubert, passed away in 1935.

He was 53 years old when he passed away on December 1, 1958.

THOMAS COMPEAU[34]

Thomas passed away on December 1, 1958.

SISTER LOUISE DUNN[35]

Louise was born on July 22, 1933.

She was not yet a year old when the Dionne Quintuplets were born in 1934.

Louise was 48 years old when the Canada Act was passed in 1982.

She was 85 years old when she passed away on December 27, 2018.

BISHOP REMI GAULIN[36]

Remi was born in Quebec on June 30, 1787.
He was two years old when his mother passed away in 1790.
Remi was 69 years old when he passed away on May 8, 1857.

BISHOP EDWARD JOHN HORAN[37]

E dward was born on October 26, 1817 in Quebec.
He was 49 years old when Ontario was founded on July 1, 1867.
Edward was 53 years old when British Columbia joined the confederation in 1871.

He was 57 years old when he passed away on February 15, 1875.

PATRICK HORAN[38]

Patrick was born in 1821.

He was 39 years old when he passed away on March 18, 1860.

BISHOP ALEXANDER MacDONELL[39]

Alexander was born in Scotland on July 17, 1762.

He was 22 years old when his father passed away in 1785.

Alexander was 52 years old when Napoleon Bonaparte was defeated in 1815.

He was 64 years old when his brother, Squire Allan Ban MacDonell passed away in 1826.

Alexander was 69 years old when the Scottish Reform Act was passed in 1832.

He was 77 years old when he passed away on January 14, 1840 in Scotland. Alexander was buried in Kingston, Ontario.

BISHOP JOHN O'BRIEN[40]

John was born in Ontario on February 19, 1832.

He was 34 years old when Ontario was founded on July 1, 1867.

John was 38 years old when British Columbia joined the confederation in 1871.

He was the fourth bishop of Kingston.

John was 47 years old when he passed away on August 1, 1879 in Quebec. He was buried in Kingston.

SISTER ELLEN O'DONNELL[41]

Ellen passed away on August 26, 1883.

BISHOP PATRICK PHELAN[42]

Patrick was born in Ireland on February 1, 1795. He was 62 years old when he passed away on June 7, 1857.

MARGARET POWERS[43]

Margaret was born on June 8, 1854 in Trenton, Ontario.

She was 12 years old when Ontario was founded on July 1, 1867.

Margaret was 16 years old when British Columbia joined the confederation in 1871.

She was 62 years old when she passed away on December 23, 1916.

ANDREW G. REID[44]

Andrew was born in 1923.

He was 11 years old when the Dionne Quintuplets were born in 1934.

Andrew was 39 years old when his mother passed away in 1962.

He was 53 years old when he passed away on April 13, 1973.

SISTER JULIA STAFFORD[45]

Julia was born in Drummond, Ontario in 1844.

She was 22 years old when her father passed away in 1866.

Julia was 26 years old when British Columbia joined the confederation in 1871.

She was 42 years old when she passed away on May 22, 1886.

[1] https://www.wikitree.com/genealogy/Heffner-Family-Tree-282

[2] https://www.wikitree.com/genealogy/Buck-Family-Tree-5885

[3] https://www.wikitree.com/genealogy/Buck-Family-Tree-5884

[4] https://www.wikitree.com/genealogy/Fairbanks-Family-Tree-709

[5] https://www.wikitree.com/genealogy/Fairbanks-Family-Tree-1122

[6] https://www.wikitree.com/genealogy/McLeod-Family-Tree-4983

[7] https://www.wikitree.com/genealogy/Bedard-Family-Tree-1248

[8] https://www.wikitree.com/genealogy/Perry-Family-Tree-15411

[9] https://www.wikitree.com/genealogy/Glazeby-Family-Tree-1

[10] https://www.wikitree.com/genealogy/Wellborn-Family-Tree-280

[11] https://www.wikitree.com/genealogy/Wellborn-Family-Tree-350

[12] https://www.wikitree.com/genealogy/Ranson-Family-Tree-198

[13] https://www.wikitree.com/genealogy/Hawkins-Family-Tree-16698

[14] https://www.wikitree.com/genealogy/Udell-Family-Tree-38

[15] https://www.wikitree.com/genealogy/Lester-Family-Tree-3962

[16] https://www.wikitree.com/genealogy/Fowler-Family-Tree-16196

[17] https://www.wikitree.com/genealogy/Fowler-Family-Tree-16197

[18] https://www.wikitree.com/genealogy/Fowler-Family-Tree-12980

[19] https://www.wikitree.com/genealogy/Fowler-Family-Tree-16198

[20] https://www.wikitree.com/genealogy/O'Connor-Family-Tree-6726

[21] https://www.wikitree.com/genealogy/Austin-Family-Tree-15005

[22] https://www.wikitree.com/genealogy/Brazzoni-Family-Tree-3

[23] https://www.wikitree.com/genealogy/Compeau-Family-Tree-82

[24] https://www.wikitree.com/genealogy/Buck-Family-Tree-8611

[25] https://www.wikitree.com/genealogy/Byrne-Family-Tree-6335

[26] https://www.wikitree.com/genealogy/Byrne-Family-Tree-6336

[27] https://www.wikitree.com/genealogy/Campbell-Family-Tree-54480

[28] https://www.wikitree.com/genealogy/Tisdale-Family-Tree-1343

[29] https://www.wikitree.com/genealogy/Cleary-Family-Tree-2489

[30] https://www.wikitree.com/genealogy/Compeau-Family-Tree-83

[31] https://www.wikitree.com/genealogy/Compeau-Family-Tree-84

[32] https://www.wikitree.com/genealogy/Tisdale-Family-Tree-1346

[33] https://www.wikitree.com/genealogy/Compeau-Family-Tree-85

[34] https://www.wikitree.com/genealogy/Compeau-Family-Tree-86

[35] https://www.wikitree.com/genealogy/Dunn-Family-Tree-19606

[36] https://www.wikitree.com/genealogy/Gaulin-Family-Tree-206

[37] https://www.wikitree.com/genealogy/Horan-Family-Tree-950

[38] https://www.wikitree.com/genealogy/Horan-Family-Tree-951

[39] https://www.wikitree.com/genealogy/Macdonell-Family-Tree-246

[40] https://www.wikitree.com/genealogy/O'Brien-Family-Tree-12600

[41] https://www.wikitree.com/genealogy/O'Donnell-Family-Tree-4386

[42] https://www.wikitree.com/genealogy/Phelan-Family-Tree-146

[43] https://www.wikitree.com/genealogy/Powers-Family-Tree-9311

[44] https://www.wikitree.com/genealogy/Reid-Family-Tree-20101

[45] https://www.wikitree.com/genealogy/Stafford-Family-Tree-7500

Don't miss out!

Visit the website below and you can sign up to receive emails whenever Angeline Gallant publishes a new book. There's no charge and no obligation.

https://books2read.com/r/B-A-QGSI-KMJBC

BOOKS 2 READ

Connecting independent readers to independent writers.

Also by Angeline Gallant

Calling Her Heart
Whisper of the Heart
No Turning Back
Forsake Me Not
Hear My Cry

Keeper Of Secrets
A Lady's Secret

Midnight's Awakening
Heart of the Storm
Walking Through The Storm

Secrets of the Underworld
Deklan's Dragons

Tell My Story Collection

Tell My Story: England 1852

The Grave Whisperer
Wedding Bells in Kingston, Ontario, Canada 1923
St. Paul's Anglican Churchyard Kingston, Ontario, Canada A-B
St. Paul's Anglican Churchyard, Kingston, Ontario, Canada C - D
St. Paul's Anglican Churchyard, Kingston, Ontario, Canada G - H
St. Paul's Anglican Churchyard, Kingston, Ontario, Canada J - N
St. Paul's Anglican Churchyard, Kingston, Ontario, Canada O - R
St. Paul's Anglican Churchyard, Kingston, Ontario, Canada S - T
St. Paul's Anglican Churchyard, Kingston, Ontario T - Z
Small Graveyards & Burial Grounds: Kingston, Ontario, Canada

The Wolf Whisperer Series
The Cry of the Wolf
Journey of the Heart
Wolf Whisperer volumes 1 & 2

Standalone
Winds of Change vol 1-3

Watch for more at https://www.goodreads.com/author/show/
19703964.Angeline_Gallant.